ADAM'S AMAZING EARTH SUIT

Copyright © 2015 Joy Buckley.

All rights reserved. No part of this book may be used or reproduced by any means, graphic, electronic, or mechanical, including photocopying, recording, taping or by any information storage retrieval system without the written permission of the publisher except in the case of brief quotations embodied in critical articles and reviews.

Balboa Press books may be ordered through booksellers or by contacting:

Balboa Press
A Division of Hay House
1663 Liberty Drive
Bloomington, IN 47403
www.balboapress.com
1 (877) 407-4847

Because of the dynamic nature of the Internet, any web addresses or links contained in this book may have changed since publication and may no longer be valid. The views expressed in this work are solely those of the author and do not necessarily reflect the views of the publisher, and the publisher hereby disclaims any responsibility for them.

Any people depicted in stock imagery provided by Thinkstock are models,
and such images are being used for illustrative purposes only.
Certain stock imagery © Thinkstock.

ISBN: 978-1-5043-2661-2 (sc)
ISBN: 978-1-5043-2662-9 (e)

Library of Congress Control Number: 2015900554

Print information available on the last page.

Balboa Press rev. date: 06/12/2015

Dedicated to Lucca Jazz Winston, who taught me how to laugh and Susan Marie Getlein, who taught me how to love.

Mary Getlein

Dedicated to Lucca Jazz Winston, who asked the questions that made this book possible.

Joy Buckley

Written by Joy Buckley
Illustrated by Mary Getlein

Hello, my name is Adam. Once I was invisible. I was pure energy. I zoomed all over the place. I could do lots of things but I could not eat ice cream or play with toys, I really wanted to see what that would be like.

Where I lived, if you wished very hard, your wish would come true. My mind told me that all I needed to do was to find an Earth Suit and put it on. Where would I find an Earth Suit? Why, on Earth, of course!

There, the Mamas make Earth Suits in their tummies. At first my suit was very tiny but after I put it on, it started to grow. When it fit just right, I was born!

My suit was made of stretchy skin and I could make it move. It took a while to get it to do what I wanted. It was kind of tight but it kept stretching. I learned to talk and to play. I loved to eat ice cream.

Sometimes I would get a rip in my Earth Suit and Mama would patch it up with a Band-Aid. Did that ever happen to you? Earth suits don't last forever, you know, so you have to take good care of them. There are baths to take, teeth to scrub, hair to shampoo and healthy foods to eat.

I kept growing and my suit kept stretching, bigger and bigger. One day, I was as tall as I would ever be. I was a grown up! I could do so many things.

I could drive a car and go wherever I wanted to go with my friends.

I could rescue a cat and name him, Bingo.

I could plant a garden and grow yummy vegetables to eat.

Many years passed and something began to happen. My hair turned gray and I started to shrink a little. My Earth Suit started to sag and I saw some wrinkles in it.

My suit was wearing out, soon I would have to take it off and go back to being pure energy. I had fun on Earth. Now, it was time to go. One day, I laid my Earth Suit down and jumped out of it.

I was invisible again. Everybody thought I was gone but I was right there. Someday I may find a brand new Earth Suit so everyone can see me again.

But, for now, I'll say… I'll be seeing you.

Imagine and Draw Your "Pure Energy"

Got a different version of Your "Pure Energy"? Imagine and draw.

Imagine and Draw a Family members "Pure Energy"

Imagine and Draw a Family members "Pure Energy"

Imagine and Draw a Family members "Pure Energy"

Imagine and Draw a Friends "Pure Energy"

Imagine and Draw a Pets "Pure Energy"

CPSIA information can be obtained at www.ICGtesting.com
Printed in the USA
BVIW12s1612170918
R9091400003B/7